JOSHUA TREE
desert reflections

by Stephen Trimble

with sidebar essays by Joe Zarki,
Chief of Interpretation
Joshua Tree National Park

published by
Joshua Tree National Park Association

JOSHUA TREE NATIONAL PARK

desert magic—a vibration communicated in warm earth colors through clean, bright air and great open spaces. This magic is elusive, a simple, silent message too complicated for words, but quietly revealed by every rugged landscape, every hardy plant. Clear light shines everywhere, pigments of dawn and day and dusk coloring a cloudless sky, an airy dome of desert light.

Dawn. The luminous, pale moon sinks behind mountain rock. Bunchgrass glows with the first touch of sun, creatures of the night scatter toward burrows, daytime animals stir from their rest.

Joshua Tree National Park preserves a part

CONTENTS

From the largest desert mammal, bighorn sheep, to the blossoming datura, the life force of the desert is palpable.

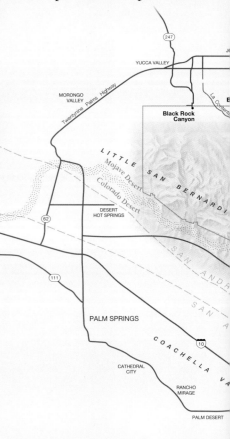

of this magical desert world, a wild place of unexpected variety. Tiptoe here past mule deer to the rims of sheer mountain cliffs, or lie under swaying palms in the soothing shade and green of an oasis. Wander under an erratic lace canopy of Joshua tree limbs, or scramble like bighorn sheep to the tops of jumbled rockpiles.

A reality that doesn't match the classic image of deserts? The expected extremes are here, too: the pure desertness of sandy flats and sidewinders, heat-blistered arroyos and cactus-studded bajadas.

Indian, prospector, and cowboy preceded us. But only a few. This land makes a challenging home, and the enterprising people who lived here for a time moved on. They left a wilderness, a world tuned to natural cadences.

We come to this place to share in its peace, to listen to its stories, to glory at its beauty. Whenever we leave, the desert beckons us back with the tantalizing shimmer of freedom.

The pulse of life at Joshua Tree beats to the rhythm of the seasons, the daily cycle of the sun. Water—mostly the lack of it—sets the tempo. Drought slows the desert to a near halt, while rain sparks new life. With patience, and sometimes passion, the desert abides.

Though humans have tried to lay claim to this rugged land, kestrels may have a more lasting presence.

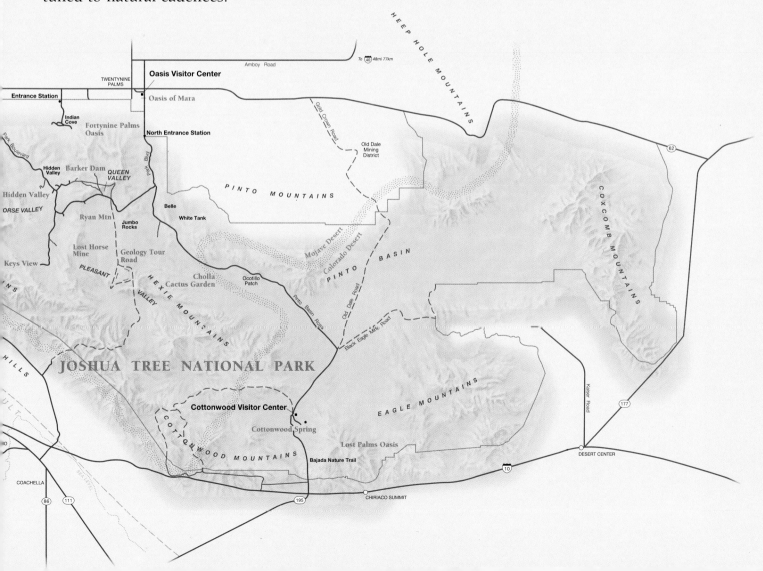

of rocks and joshua trees

High desert valleys in Joshua Tree National Park bristle with a forest of dagger-leaved Joshua trees, the unforgettable symbols of this arid landscape. Every road in the park's high desert passes through these eerie forests, where at the far edges of valleys the distant Joshua trees merge in a spiny, spidery haze. Mountains provide a backdrop, jumbles of rounded boulders an accent, but the Joshua trees dominate this land.

Legend has it that Mormon pioneers gave the Joshua trees their name. In the branching shape of this tree, these thirsty desert travelers saw the prophet Joshua waving them on, leading them toward the Promised Land with upraised arms.

Other early visitors to Joshua tree country found the spiny tree less welcome in appearance: they called the giant yucca "grotesque," "tormented," and "repulsive." Even those who find Joshua trees bizarre will admit that these great yuccas give this land its unique personality. Joshua Tree narrowly missed being called Desert Plants National Monument. The name that won out suits this desert, for of all its remarkable plants, Joshua trees linger in memory as the most remarkable.

WORLD OF THE JOSHUA TREE
Most Joshua trees grow wild in the Mojave Desert. Their southernmost stand—here in Joshua Tree National Park—marks the transition from the Mojave Desert to the Colorado Desert (a part of the larger Sonoran Desert).

In spring, a cluster of creamy blossoms tips many angular branches. Not all Joshua trees bloom every year, but in some years flowering is spectacular. The leathery, bell-shaped blossoms for years have challenged botanists trying to

Mountains provide a backdrop, jumbles of rocks an accent, but the Joshua trees dominate this land.

The omnivorous coyote, desert totem, flourishes in the Joshua tree environment.

classify Joshua trees. Some experts place Joshua trees among the agaves; some group Joshua trees and other yuccas in the lily family.

With the Joshua tree grows Mojave yucca, though the latter also grows abundantly in the low desert, where no Joshua trees occur. Mojave yuccas resemble their more thickly branched, larger relatives, the Joshua trees, but have white fibers edging their longer leaves, in contrast to the Joshua trees' shorter, minutely toothed leaves.

gnawed off the rigid, needle-tipped swords to armor their nests. These leaves, combined with well-placed clusters of cactus spines, discourage all but the most dedicated coyote or badger in search of a wood rat dinner.

When the Joshua trees bloom, their flowers provide tender, moist feasting for Beechey ground squirrels, for birds, and even for deer. Later, the fleshy fruits, and still later, the dry seeds, reward antelope ground squirrels and other animals in their search for food.

Many years pass before Joshua trees accumulate enough branches to look truly distinguished. Joshua trees may live 20 years before they branch and flower for the first time. The mazelike form of a big tree identifies it as a centuries-old elder. Where Joshua trees struggle to live with extreme aridity, rocky soil, or cold winters, they grow slowly and rarely flower. Here, small trees with few branches may be very old.

Without the key resource of Joshua trees, many animals would lack the food and shelter they need to survive. In the giant yucca forest, stubs of Joshua tree leaves show where wood rats have

Here, where other trees are few, Joshua trees provide crucial nesting places for birds. Woodpeckers drill holes in the trunks which screech owls sometimes use after the woodpeckers have moved on. Scott's orioles weave their pouched nests in the shade of Joshua tree leaf clusters. Both the woodpecker and oriole glean much of their insect food from the trunk and leaves of their Joshua tree home.

Scavengers need a clear view, and ravens often pause atop Joshua trees when not soaring high over the desert. The twenty, or even forty-foot height of a Joshua tree makes a useful perch for kestrels and loggerhead shrikes as well. These birds poise on high branches to await the flash of an unsuspecting grasshopper or side-blotched lizard. Lacking talons, shrikes skewer their prey on thorns and barbed wire. Lizard carcasses impaled on the tips of Joshua tree leaves track their meals.

Joshua trees favor sandy soil where they can spread their moisture-seeking roots in a dense network. The root system does not reach deep enough,

rely on the female yucca moth for pollination. No other animal visiting the flowers transfers the pollen necessary for seed formation from one flower to another. Though a Joshua tree sometimes can sprout new plants from its roots, only the seeds it produces in pollinated flowers can scatter far enough to establish Joshua trees in new areas.

Most plants have evolved flowers that "accidentally" capture pollen carried by a moth (or other insect, bird, or bat) intent only on eating nectar. But the yucca

however, to prevent occasional toppling of trees in high winds. Downed trees make homes for the desert night lizard, which prefers these dead branches to all other places.

Turning over a dead limb or two may reveal this shy reptile, along with its diet of termites, ants, beetles, flies, spiders, and maybe a scorpion. This thin-skinned lizard, easily dried by the sun, has met the challenge of the desert by totally avoiding this land's harshest extremes. Unlike most North American desert lizards, it waits out hot daytime hours in moist hiding places of dead trees, saving its energy for the cool, more humid night.

THE MOTH AND THE GIANT YUCCA

Though some of these animals would find it difficult to live without the Joshua tree, the giant yucca could survive nicely without all but one of the animals. Only the yucca moth has evolved a life cycle so closely tied to the Joshua tree that one cannot exist without the other.

Joshua trees (and most other yuccas)

moth need not be enticed to leave its pollen. On the contrary, the female moth has evolved special organs with which she collects pollen. She then carefully spreads her hoard of pollen onto the receptive surface of the flower.

No other known insect pollinates flowers so deliberately. Though the moth seems to understand the mechanics of plant reproduction, she also has her own reasons for her careful pollination rites. She lays eggs in the flower's ovary, and when the larvae hatch they feed on the seeds. Without pollination, moth larvae would have no seeds to eat. They eat only a few of the dozens of seeds, however, leaving plenty to shake free from the fruit as the wind tumbles it across the desert.

Holes pepper a dry Joshua tree seed pod in fall where the moth larvae drill through the papery husk to emerge, dropping to the ground to spin their cocoons. Every pod with seeds has these holes, since without a visit by an egg-laying moth, no seeds can develop.

The moth eats neither nectar nor pol-

Antelope ground squirrels find abundant fruits and seeds in the shadows of the Joshua trees, while predators like badgers and screech owls hunt in those same shadows.

len. Her step-by-step actions seem to have no function other than to fertilize the flower, insuring food for young she never sees and survival for her species.

How did this amazing partnership evolve? Though we have no answer, in these two intertwined lives the desert reveals one of the complexities hidden by its simple surface, and shares an inconspicuous event full of mystery.

Most yuccas rely exclusively on the tiny female yucca moth for pollination; in a reciprocal arrangement, the moth's eggs are laid in the yucca flower, their larvae feed on the seeds—and the remaining seeds rejuvenate the yucca population.

ROCKPILES Second only to Joshua trees among the most memorable images in the park are great heaps of boulders, eroded in a fantastic variety of arches, windows, knobs, and hollows. Rockpiles and Joshua trees complement each other and combine to distinguish the high desert from the low desert below and the mountains above.

Rockpiles rise from the flats of Queen and Lost Horse Valleys, pink rock sculptures scattered among thorny desert plants. A close look at the valley soils discloses simply a sandy, gravelly version of the rock that juts above. Why do the rockpiles remain higher than the valleys when both consist of the same rock? Why hasn't erosion worn them to the same level as the valley floor?

To answer these questions, forget the present—it exists as hardly a fraction of an instant in the incredibly long span of time outlined in the rocks. Cease thinking in lifetimes; plunge back in the Earth's history millions of years—long before humans. Here, more than 80 million years ago, the rock that now forms Jumbo Rocks and Indian Cove oozed upward from the inner earth as molten liquid. Similar outcroppings just east of Indian Cove date to 245 million years ago. These mobile bodies of rock did not reach the surface but cooled below ground and crystallized to igneous rocks called quartz monzonite and monzogranite—different types of granite.

In the millions of years that followed, gradual uplift of this part of the Earth's crust forced the erosion and stripping away of many thousands of feet of the ancient rock that had covered the quartz monzogranite. This unimaginably slow sequence of events brought

The dramatic rockpiles of Queen and Lost Horse valleys expose corestones eroded mostly below ground, the last remnants of larger blocks softened and rounded before finally being exposed.

the granitic rock to the surface. In the layer of monzogranite just beneath the surface, groundwater seeped downward along joints, the horizontal and vertical sets of fractures in rock that divide it into blocks. This water began chemically transforming hard mineral grains along its path into soft clay, while it loosened and freed grains resistant to solution. (see figure 1)

Where two joints intersected, alteration of mineral grains at block edges went twice as fast. At corners, water

could reach fresh rock along three joints: with time, this intense action at corners —three times as effective as alteration on block sides—rounded the blocks. Rectangular stones slowly weathered to spheres of hard rock surrounded by newly formed soft clay containing countless loose mineral grains. This long process took place when Joshua Tree had a much wetter climate than today. (see figure 2)

Finally, with the arrival of the arid climate of recent times, the violent attack of desert flash floods began to slice through the old protective ground surface, washing away clay and loose mineral grains along joints, and gradually lowering the surface level of the valley. These powerful floodwaters exposed spherical cores of intact, undecomposed rock remaining in the centers of each block isolated by joints.

Gradual, continual washing away of soft clay and loosened mineral grains left the deepest blocks—those not yet completely isolated—standing high above the new valley floor. Smaller, isolated block remnants form piles of spherical boulders at their bases. (see figure 3)

Eventually, at the very end of this long story, humans arrived to wonder at the origin of these huge jumbles of rounded rocks—and to climb them. We might have guessed rockpiles on the high desert were created solely by today's desert winds and flash floods. But these "jumbo rocks" are ancient, a fossil landscape blocked out in the earth millions of years ago, with edges softened and rounded below ground during the thousands of years before today's deserts were formed.

THE HIDDEN VALLEY RUSTLERS Early

desert explorers favored the least rugged, best-watered travel routes they could find. To pass from Los Angeles eastward across the desert, they followed the Mojave River, which led them through Cajon Pass. The easier route between the great walls of the San Jacinto and San Bernardino Mountains—San Gorgonio Pass—saw less pioneer traffic because it lacked the river.

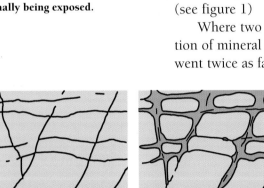
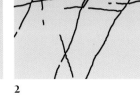
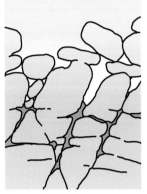

1   2   3

Joshua Tree National Park is a rock climber's paradise— nearly a quarter of a million climbers come here annually to match their skills against the challenge and extreme beauty of this landscape.

The golden land of California passed from the hands of Spain to Mexico to the United States before travelers began to branch off in numbers from the trail down San Gorgonio Pass through the Coachella Valley. Not until the 1850s did the newcomers follow the old Indian trails through the natural passage up Morongo Valley and past Twentynine Palms toward Arizona.

By the 1870s, prospectors roamed the high desert mountains, and ranchers began running their cows in the high desert valleys. The following decades proved the land prime cattle country, high enough in elevation to receive the rainfall needed for lush growth of galleta and desert needlegrass, the bunchgrasses

Dams constructed in natural drainages store floodwaters as water sources for livestock. Barker Dam began as one of these "tanks"—the most conspicuous legacy of the early cattlemen in the Joshua Tree desert.

that color the desert floor. Joshua trees and rockpiles may define the personality of the high desert, but grass attracted the first significant pioneers.

Among the first to take advantage of Joshua Tree rangeland were Jim and Bill McHaney, the legendary rustlers of Hidden Valley. These brothers arrived by 1879, and local tradition paints them as leaders of the McHaney Gang, driving stolen cattle into the high desert for rebranding before moving them on to the coast to be sold. Isolated Hidden Valley and the Wonderland of Rocks made tempting natural corrals for their herds.

Other cattlemen followed the McHaneys into the desert. Tanks (dams in natural drainages constructed by the ranchers to catch floodwaters) are their most conspicuous legacy. Barker Dam, White Tank, Squaw Tank, Live Oak Tank—all began as waterholes for cattle.

Drought, combined with grazing restrictions set after establishment of the park as a reserve, brought the Joshua Tree cattle industry to an end in the 1940s. Tanks that remain intact today trap water critical for desert bighorn sheep and other wildlife. Their wind-rippled surfaces reflect an ever-changing desert: passing seasons and colors, sun-warmed rocks, and glimpses of the people who come to visit.

Riding the high desert, cattlemen found their eyes wandering upward to the ridges of mountains that border the valleys. Many found themselves lured away from ranching and into these mountains, for hidden in them lies the second resource that drew men to this land—gold.

To trace this page in Joshua Tree's history we must leave the picturesque high valleys behind. With pick and shovel, leading a trusty burro, tramp along with the fabled and timeless prospector into the desert mountains.

In the spring of 1999, following the unforgettable bloom of the previous year, the desert was parched. A series of lightning strikes just before Memorial Day weekend started a series of small blazes that soon grew into a single large fire called the Juniper Complex. Before the fire burned itself out it had consumed 14,000 acres of park.

The assessment of the Juniper Complex fires, the largest in park history, revealed a disturbing trend. Wildfires had been increasing in size and intensity in the park for a number of years. Exotic grasses had spread dramatically during the same period.

Most scientists believed that, historically, wildfires were rare events in desert landscapes. Native grasses in Joshua Tree are for the most part bunch grasses that grow in scattered clusters, too sparse to carry fire. The addition of exotic grasses has changed this pattern.

Alien grass species, mostly in the genus *Bromus,* now occupy large swaths of the Mojave Desert portion of the park. Unlike the scattered bunch grasses, bromes grow in carpets, often in the shade of larger trees or shrubs. Once they dry out, these invaders create enough fine fuel to easily ignite and carry fire.

Blackbrush, junipers, piñon pines, scrub oaks, and Joshua trees are native species that will burn under the right conditions. The increased frequency of wildfires has converted some desert woodlands to grasslands and other annual plants that are much more likely to burn in the future. It is uncertain if the native trees and shrubs can ever successfully re-establish themselves once fire has removed them.

Most of what is known about fire in natural landscapes has come from studies done in forests and grasslands. There, the impact of fire on timber and grazing provided the economic incentive for scientists and land managers to carry out the long-term studies needed to develop better wildfire policies and practices. Ecologists now know that many wildland habitats have evolved in the presence of fire, and the health of these ecosystems declines when fire is suppressed.

Much less is known about the role of fire in desert landscapes. The conventional wisdom that periodic wildfires are largely beneficial in nature may not be true in the desert. Will there be Joshua trees in the park's future? To answer this question managers need a better understanding of the interplay among fire, exotic grasses, and native desert vegetation.

MOUNTAINS
crossroads of change

Jim and Bill McHaney had been running cattle in Joshua Tree's high valleys for more than fifteen years when a neighbor struck gold at Queen Mountain. The Desert Queen Mine seemed a rich strike, and the McHaneys had grown a bit possessive of their high desert home. By 1895, the mine passed into the hands of the McHaney Gang after the previous owner of the Desert Queen died in a gunfight that looked suspiciously like an ambush.

Murder charges were impossible to prove, but the shooting of the Desert Queen's discoverer added one more sensational tale to the rustlers' fierce reputation. Desert mountain mines seem to breed such legends. Lost treasure, murder, and dreams of fabulous wealth all color the stories of the Southwest's champion wanderers: the prospectors.

Many improvised claim markers, like this one near the Mastodon Mine, attest to the "gold fever" that brought hundreds of prospectors to the region. Legal mining claims filed with county recorders provided better protection from claim jumpers.

THE LOST HORSE & THE DESERT QUEEN

In the early 1860s, a claim in the mountains just south of Twentynine Palms Oasis brought miners to the area. The next big strike, in dry, wild country a few miles east, blossomed into the region's biggest producer of gold. From the 1880s through the First World War the Virginia Dale district

Notice of Location

QUARTZ CLAIM

Notice is hereby Given: That .... the undersigned, States, having made discovery of mineral and rock in place, right of discovery and location, the within mentioned Qua... upon the discovery monument have posted a duplicate not... Notice of its location in accordance with the U. S. Revised St... laws and customs, and with the rules and regulations of th... measurement of this claim is .... linear feet, in leng... ment, and the ....erly end line is .... feet ....erly from covery monument, and said end line is .... erly erly side, ...erly and said ...d lines are pa.... feet of the said quartz lode, vein, ledge or deposit, and it is more cribed as follows: Commencing at A stone monument in a N. Westerly direction from the discovery monument, ...

(named after its first mine) drew miners into the mountains. Their boomtowns followed from strike to strike: Old Dale disappeared and the saloons and cabins of New Dale moved cross-country with the miners.

Civilization had a difficult time keeping up with miners in the West, for they moved on soon after making any strike that created a new boomtown. Most cared more for the search than the goal. Once they located rich ore, they sold out fast and disappeared over the next ridge, claiming to be on the trail of an even bigger strike. Though they insisted that gold fueled their dreams, perhaps

its discoverer—who had found it while searching for his lost horse.

Whichever lost horse led the way, gold convinced miners to stay. Johnny Lang, and later the Ryan family, sank a shaft deep into the flanks of Lost Horse Mountain and eventually shipped out millions of dollars in bullion. To crush the ore, they built a mill that smashed rock to powder with ten 850-pound "stamps." To extract gold from the powdered rock, miners captured the fine yellow particles in a mercury compound (or later, in a cyanide solution), and then isolated the gold from this mixture. Rock dust remaining after refining accumulated in piles of tailings

Historic El Dorado Mine.

the prospectors simply craved the feel of solitary living in the desert wilderness. Maybe they gloried most in knowing they left behind legends.

These local yarns tangle the facts surrounding the discovery of the Lost Horse Mine. In one story, a cowboy named Johnny Lang found rich ore while searching for a lost horse; another version accuses the McHaney Gang of stealing Johnny's horses while he and his partners staked out their claim. Still another maintains that Johnny bought the claim from

surrounding the mill. Today, much of the Lost Horse stamp mill remains standing, an impressive relic of the labor of dozens of dreamers.

Meanwhile, the McHaneys had run through a small fortune, gone bankrupt, and lost the Desert Queen Mine. Jim McHaney moved on to counterfeiting and ended up in prison, while his brother Bill took to prospecting full-time. Bill was still searching for another big strike when he died in 1937, by then revered as a lovable character and important pioneer.

By the time William Keys arrived around 1910, an absentee owner ran the Desert Queen Mine. Bill hired on as watchman and inherited the mine as payment for back wages when the owner died. Bill homesteaded the old McHaney cow camp and finished his first house there in 1917. Right up to his death in 1969 he lived in the high desert with a sense of permanence felt by few other miners.

He and his wife Frances raised five children. They irrigated gardens and orchards with water from their reservoir, raised livestock, established a school at the ranch, and housed a stream of visitors. But Bill's first love was mining, and

William Keys inherited the Desert Queen Mine in the early 1900s and ingeniously transformed the old McHaney cow camp into a livable homestead for his family. No piece of old mining equipment was abandoned—a cyanide tank became the chicken coop, an old tractor a woodcutting machine.

eventually he acquired more than twenty claims in the mountains of Joshua Tree. Leasing these claims provided much of his income. As each mining company went broke, he gathered up abandoned equipment to improvise chicken coops from cyanide tanks, woodcutting machines from tractors.

In the 1940s, a feud over use of a road leading to Bill's stamp mill erupted in a gunfight with his ornery neighbor, Worth Bagley. Bill was ambushed, but proved the better shot, and Bagley bit the dust. Only

Bill witnessed the killing, and as a result he spent five years in prison before a thorough investigation, initiated by writer Erle Stanley Gardner, led to Bill's full pardon. He returned to the ranch in the desert he loved, to live for twenty years until his death at the age of 89.

Today, the National Park Service preserves the ranch as Bill left it. His life bridged the long span of Joshua Tree history from Bill McHaney's days to the crowding of the desert wilderness by thousands of weekending city folks.

Tours of Keys' Desert Queen Ranch provide a glimpse of the emotions of a family adapting to a desert of rugged mountains, isolation, and wild beauty. It took a family with the Keys' energy and ingenuity to make that life a success. Their departure left the desert silent once more. With a mining scar here and there, minus a few Joshua trees removed for fuel, the desert is still a wilderness.

MOUNTAIN CROSSROADS Stand at Keys View in the coolness of the early morning wind. This perch near the summit of the Little San Bernardino Mountains, nearly a mile high, reaches barely halfway up the mountains across the great low basin of the Coachella Valley, where the San Jacinto Range towers to an abrupt horizon almost 11,000 feet high.

The deep valley below sinks southward to the pale blue sheen of the Salton Sea, 235 feet below sea level. The wall of the San Jacintos ends to the right at the windy slot of San Gorgonio Pass, where the San Bernardino Mountains plunge down to the pass from the north. The high point of the San Bernardinos glints with the sparkle of snow even into summer—11,502-foot San Gorgonio Mountain. Years ago, Bill Keys built the road to this viewpoint; he could have picked no finer spot for admiring a sweep of desert country where the continent churns with tectonic activity.

Here you stand at the geographic crossroads of southern California. The San Jacintos across the valley lead south toward Mexico. The Salton Sea shimmers in a trough that forms the emerged northern extension of the Gulf of California; as far inland as Indio, immediately downslope, the land lies below sea level.

The Little San Bernardinos, and the

From Keys View near the summit of the Little San Bernardino Mountains, the San Jacinto Range rises 11,000 feet above the Coachella Valley floor.

the incredible changing park

Minerva Hoyt's success in persuading Franklin Roosevelt to set aside Joshua Tree National Monument ironically did not provide the permanent protection that the "Apostle of the Cacti" sought for her beloved desert. In fact, almost from the park's designation in August 1936

mining interests challenged the grand-scale park that Mrs. Hoyt had fought for.

The mining industry, business groups, and local governments had long argued that there were important mineral deposits in the area. At the time the national monument was established some 8,800

mining claims existed in the monument, most in the eastern half where the ore deposits offered greater potential for commercial development. Four months after the monument's designation, the California state mineralogist insisted it should be reopened for mining, "otherwise the State of California and

the nation will lose much by the retarded development of the valuable mineral resources of the area involved."

Agitation by mining organizations led Congressman Harry R. Sheppard of California to introduce legislation in 1939 to extend the mining laws throughout Joshua Tree National Monument. The first park superintendent, James Cole, worked

quietly to persuade some organizations to withdraw their support for the bill. Other groups continued to advocate that mining should be allowed for strategic defense minerals. The presence of rich iron deposits in the Eagle Mountains had been known since the 1890s, and this iron, it was argued, could support a thriving Pacific shipbuilding industry.

The war brought about shortages of manpower and equipment, but in 1946 Congressman Sheppard again introduced legislation that sought to reduce the boundaries of the park by eliminating the eastern section so prized by the mining industry.

Sheppard's bill was opposed by some miners who would settle for nothing less than opening the entire monument to miner-

al entry. Sheppard re-introduced his bill the following year seeking to reduce the park by 300,000 acres; however, it was a companion bill by Congressman John Phillips that finally passed on September 25, 1950. Prominently missing from the bill was a provision to allow mining in the remaining monument lands. The final cutback of 280,324 acres left a 557,934-acre monument. Passage of the 1994

California Desert Protection Act restored many of these lands to the renamed and expanded Joshua Tree National Park, bringing it to its present 794,000-acre size.

1946 1950 1994

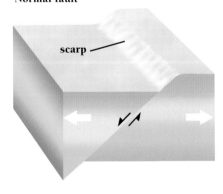

The San Andreas Fault passes through the Coachella Valley on its east-west bend near Joshua Tree National Park.

The scars left by displacement along faults can be seen in the landscape as "scarps." The Pinto Mountain Fault scarp is visible at the Oasis of Mara in Twentynine Palms.

Eagle Mountains just to the east, form the eastern end of a narrow mountainous belt that cuts across nearly all of southern California. This band of ranges starts at the coast and ends here at Joshua Tree, where the mountains form a high, transverse barrier (hence, their official designation, the Transverse Ranges) between the Mojave Desert to the north and the fiercely arid Colorado Desert sweeping away below Keys View.

These steep-walled mountain ranges formed along faults, great fractures in the Earth's crust. At these faults, movement occurs to release the enormous stresses built up through constant pushing, stretching, and wrenching of the brittle shell of the Earth—movements that eventually leave mountains standing high above basins.

People feel tremors only from the largest, most abrupt slips along faults (we call them earthquakes), but smaller movements occur frequently. The most active of all America's faults, the San Andreas, runs from the Salton Sea through the Coachella Valley and north for six hundred miles, beyond San Francisco. Jostling, shearing movements along branches of this fault created the panorama at Keys View and such movements continue today, gradually increasing the height of the viewpoint above the Salton trough far below.

Even these mountains of rock could

disappear, whittled away by erosion. That they haven't testifies to continuing movement along the faults which created them, and to their hardness. The ancient rock that covered the quartz monzogranite has not disappeared completely: Joshua Tree's mountains preserve great masses of this rock, among the oldest rocks in California, towering above the younger monzogranite.

Long ago, immense pressure and heat welded layers of ancient sedimentary rock into new, stronger rock—transformed it into the metamorphic rock we formerly called Pinto gneiss, but now divide into a complex of four subunits widely distributed in California's Transverse Ranges. This transformation of sedimentary layers took place as long as 1.7 billion years ago. The environments that formed these sediments lie so far back in the dim reaches of the Earth's beginnings that we know next to nothing about them.

We can separate metamorphic gneiss from the younger monzogranite at a glance. Dark gray, with arching bands of light-colored quartz, the mountains loom over the pink granitic rockpiles as

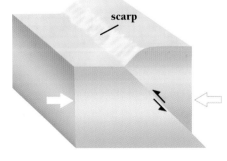

shadowed masses of twisted rock. Even without knowing that the gneiss predates the quartz monzogranite, we might have guessed it from the dark immensity of peaks in the Pintos and Little San Bernardinos: they *look* old.

CANYON AND WOODLAND These mountains sweeping eastward into the desert bring a bit of coastal California with them. In the cool, moist, upper reaches of the Little San Bernardino and Eagle Mountains, pockets of shrubby chaparral —scrub oak and red-barked manzanita— provide food and cover for scrub jays and mountain quail.

These high, rocky slopes yield to the sparing green touch of singleleaf piñons and California junipers, trees which

Within the woodland of singleleaf piñon pine and California juniper, gray fox hunt piñon mice. In the rocky canyons, chuckwalla bask amid hardy plants like Parry nolina.

form a woodland home for a group of distinctive Southwestern animals. A few mule deer browse through shrubs while bushtits and oak titmice fly after insects in scaly juniper foliage. Piñon nuts are a staple food for Merriam chipmunks and piñon jays. The smallest rodents provide food for red coachwhips, snakes that also eat other small mammals, birds, and lizards. In winter, dark-eyed juncos and mountain chickadees move into the woodland from the high mountains. And at night, piñon mice must look sharp to avoid the pounce of a bobcat or gray fox.

Though the familiar Joshua trees and Mojave yuccas grow here, another relative of the yucca clan, Parry nolina, joins them only at these high elevations. Nolinas bear a feathery, white flower stalk which fades to golden brown, and

have long grasslike leaves. With these spiky plants grows blackbrush, the thorny shrub that give the mountains their gray color.

Rocky canyons that plunge down through the mountains owe their existence to flash floods. If floods come frequently enough, boulder-choked barriers to travel become cleanly scoured passageways. Joshua Tree receives part of its meager precipitation all at once, in late summer thundershowers. Rain beats down on rock and runs off quickly, roaring down canyons. Most plants benefit little from this water, which soon evaporates and leaves the canyon scorched dry. A few last potholes of water persist here and there, with water-loving plants close by the more dependable pools.

In canyons in the Wonderland of Rocks, a scarlet-blossoming Mojave mound cactus graces a rock garden, presided over by a basking chuckwalla or collared lizard. A walker in Fried Liver Wash flushes a black-tailed jackrabbit from cover, its midday rest interrupted. White-throated swifts scoop up insects in high-flying sweeps through still canyon air; some scientists believe they reach 200 miles per hour. When the swifts retire at evening, western pipistrelle bats replace them, their sonar guiding them to insects. In Rattlesnake Canyon, rock wrens bounce from boulder to shaded cliff, while a canyon wren's cascading call echoes from rock walls through weathered branches of dead piñon. In winter, poorwills may hibernate, each wonderfully camouflaged bird lodged in a crevice.

A clatter of pebbles announces a bighorn ram silhouetted against the blue dome of desert sky. Substantial numbers of desert bighorn sheep live in Joshua Tree, but remain in isolated rocky canyons, rarely revealing themselves to visitors. Though rivaling camels in their ability to withstand dehydration, Joshua Tree's extremes challenge even the desert bighorn's talent for dealing with heat: the sheep must reach water every few days in summer. Preservation of safe, dependable waterholes thus becomes a key to their survival. For this reason, critical water sources are closed to overnight camping by human visitors.

Bighorn suffer little natural predation, and here in the park, with no hunting, they should thrive. But their size, ranking them among the largest North American desert mammals, disguises a delicate sensitivity to environmental disturbance. They need more than food and water to survive: they cease reproducing under stress. The effects of a single person walking through a lambing area or rutting grounds at the wrong season or time of day can be disastrous to that year's reproductive success. Visitors to watering sites during critical periods can prevent the wary sheep from drinking. Once a herd is weakened by stress, normally harmless parasites can devestate it.

As the immensity of the desert hides the complex lives of desert creatures, the magnificence of the bighorn masks its perilous position in today's ever more crowded wilderness. Only with our greatest care will the fragile ecological communities of desert mountains, and their symbol, the desert bighorn, survive.

OPPOSITE: **The rugged Coxcomb Mountains loom on the east boundary of Joshua Tree National Park.**

The Eagle Mountains (below) catch the last rays of desert sun.

Desert bighorn sheep make their homes here but must reach water every few days in summer.

land of little rain

Sparse vegetation and rising temperatures reveal the character of the low desert as you enter Pinto Basin.

Bigelow or "teddy-bear" cholla greet the dawn through a haze of heat.

The lush blossom of a beavertail cactus.

The last Joshua tree disappears in the rear view mirror, branches thrown outward in warning. Why a warning? Leave Queen Valley and arrive in Pinto Basin at midday in summer and you will see.

Round a last curve and Pinto Basin abruptly appears, a great bowl rimmed by desert mountains. The basin pulsates with heat waves that transfigure the mountains into a haze of flickering blue, transform the sea of creosote bushes into a mirage of shimmering green. With each passing mile, the temperature rises. On the floor of the basin, the full impact of the change in landscape confronts you.

The low desert experience begins with a garden of shrubby Bigelow cholla cactus. Spines as dense as fur give these chollas their teddy-bear look, but a brush with one proves the reliability of a sec-

ond nickname—jumping cholla. So easy is it to hook a spiny cactus joint in a soft leg or hand that the cacti seem fully capable of leaping at passersby.

Beyond the cholla garden stretch endless flats of creosote bush and bursage (burrobush), the shrubs so widely spaced that they cover only four percent of the ground. The harshness of this low desert contrasts unmistakably with the high desert valleys, with their clumps of bunchgrass. The warning of that last Joshua tree begins to make sense.

TWO DESERTS To make it official, this journey from high to low desert crosses the boundary between two of North America's major deserts, the Mojave and the Sonoran.

Northward lies the Mojave, the high desert, with Joshua trees growing from the park north to southern Nevada and the southwest tip of Utah. Mountains rise from basins in repeating series.

The Mojave is an upland desert: even the basins lie well above sea level, most more than 2,000 feet, though Death Valley forms a major exception. Rainfall is sparse, and comes primarily in Pacific fronts in winter, along with snow that briefly blankets valleys and dusts the giant yuccas.

As the Joshua trees disappear southward, the Mojave Desert ends and the Sonoran Desert begins. The giant cactus, the saguaro, symbolizes the Sonoran Desert, but grows solely in its eastern parts, far from Joshua Tree. Where you enter the Sonoran Desert in Pinto Basin, you penetrate its most arid subdivision, the Colorado Desert.

Only along the great river that forms its eastern boundary (and gives it its name) is the Colorado Desert favored with abundant fresh water. Much of the desert, which wraps around the head of the Gulf of California at the Colorado River Delta, lies at or below sea level, dipping lowest at the Salton Sea. The sun bakes these lowlands to near wasteland, and few large shrubs and cacti can survive the unforgiving aridity away from washes. Most of the low desert's stark plains are dotted only with creosote bush and bursage—the two most drought-tolerant perennial plants in North America. Hills and slopes look almost lush in comparison, with brittlebush and spindly ocotillos.

Most of the little rainfall the Colorado Desert receives comes in late winter and spring, when westerly winds bring Pacific moisture to the dry land. Even then, clouds lose much of their rain as they rise over the high mountains which block their path toward the desert. In late summer, a few intense thunderstorms fueled by moisture from the Gulf of Mexico penetrate westward as far as Joshua Tree, bringing another pulse of precipitation to the desert.

Though sharing many inhabitants, the Mojave and Colorado Deserts have distinctive personalities as well as different names. The low desert forces adaptation to extremes, and a surprising number of living things have solved the problems presented by these extremes in spectacular fashion.

PASSIONATE AND PATIENT PLANTS

Aridity makes deserts. This dryness results from air and ocean currents, latitude, location of mountain ranges, and many other factors. Though arctic deserts exist, most familiar deserts are hot, dry, and windblown. Living in such a land of little rain becomes a challenge for any plant or animal not adapted to chronic aridity and periodic extreme drought. This is the house of the sun, and the odds always favor the house.

Twentynine Palms receives an average annual rainfall of just over four inches. In almost one out of four days each year, the temperature climbs past 100 degrees Fahrenheit. Higher and cooler elevations in the park receive twice as much rainfall. The lowest spot in Pinto Basin, on the other hand, is even hotter and drier than Twentynine Palms.

The low desert was not always so harsh. Between five and seven thousand years ago, one of the earliest known human groups in the California desert lived along the shores of a marshy river flowing through Pinto Basin. These people made distinctive chipped points for their hunting spears, and ground on rock mortars (metates) the seeds and nuts they gathered. Eventually the climate changed, drying up their river, and the families of

The deserts of North America.

GREAT BASIN DESERT

WYOMING

NEVADA

UTAH

COLORADO

CALIFORNIA

MOHAVE DESERT

ARIZONA

Eastern Mojave Nat. Preserve

Grand Canyon Nat. Park

Joshua Tree Nat. Park

NEW MEXICO

SONORAN DESERT

Colorado Desert *(subdivision of Sonoran Desert)*

CHIHUAHUAN DESERT

MEXICO

the Pinto Culture left. Later the Serrano and Cahuilla used the low desert more as a hunting and gathering ground than a home.

Home it is, though, for many organisms. Plants here survive only if their adaptations allow them either to escape from the worst of the heat and drought or to successfully endure it. Annual plants survive through escape—as seeds that lie dormant in the soil for years until that unpredictable time when a perfect balance of rain and warm temperatures triggers their germination.

Some seeds rely on coats of growth inhibitors to prevent false starts after a single skimpy rainfall. To assure enough moisture for the young plants' survival, sprouting occurs only when sufficient rain falls to wash away these layers of chemicals. Desert dandelion and evening primrose, mallow and buckwheat, lupine and phacelia: they germinate and flower with haste, in a frenzy of blossoming that must produce seed before crucial moisture disappears once more.

Perhaps the drama of the desert's spring bloom, in contrast to its normal austerity, magnifies our emotional reaction to the incredible carpet of flowers. The annuals erupt from their dormancy with a passion, a release of energy that can't help but be contagious.

Admirers of patience over passion will find kindred souls in shrubs and trees that live through the long, unpredictable dry spells. Ocotillos drop leaves in drought, and later regrow them in a matter of days when rains return. In blossom, their flame-tipped branches, all leafy green when rains come, make them almost unrecognizable if you have seen them only in drought—a random candelabra of thorny sticks.

Other trees lose their leaves in dry spells, but even with this sacrifice they can grow only along washes where sand holds a trace more moisture. Along the banks of these dry streams grows a ragged streamside forest of palo verdes, with green bark that can take over the

a park by any other name

One of the most common questions park rangers hear from visitors is, "What's the difference between a national park and a national monument?" In a nutshell, it takes an act of Congress to establish a national park. A national monument can be designated by presidential proclamation.

On October 31, 1994, President William Clinton signed the landmark California Desert Protection Act, abolishing the old Joshua Tree National Monument and replacing it with a brand new 794,000-acre Joshua Tree National Park, which was expanded by adding 234,000 acres, many of them lands that had been removed from the national monument by Congress in 1950.

Apart from the added acres, Joshua Tree National Park benefited from the more specific and detailed language Congress provided describing significance and purpose of the new national park. The original proclamation issued by President Franklin Roosevelt in 1936 gave very little guidance to park managers as to the purpose of Joshua Tree National Monument. In describing why he was creating Joshua Tree National Monument, Roosevelt stated,

"Whereas certain public lands in the State of California contain historic and prehistoric structures, and have situated thereon various objects of historic and scientific interest…" The emphasis on historic and cultural features seems odd given that much of Mrs. Hoyt's focus was on the preservation of desert plants and landscapes. Also, the proclamation makes no mention of any specific historic or prehistoric structure. This confusion over the purpose of the original national monument was likely something of a handicap to park managers over the years.

When Congress passes legislation to establish a national park, the public debate that occurs allows for careful consideration of the purpose of the proposed park and usually results in better guidance to the National Park Service over the intent for how a park should be managed. The Desert Protection Act stated that "it is…the policy of the Congress that…appropriate public lands in the California desert be included within the National Park System… in order to:

* preserve unrivaled scenic, geologic, and wildlife values associated with these unique natural landscapes;

* perpetuate in their natural state significant and diverse ecosystems of the California desert;

* protect and preserve historical and cultural values of the California desert associated with ancient Indian cultures, patterns of westward exploration and settlement and sites exemplifying the mining, ranching, and railroading history of the Old West;

* provide opportunities public recreation, protect and interpret ecological and geological features and historic, paleontological, and archeological sites, maintain wilderness resource values, and promote public understanding and appreciation of the California desert;

* and retain and enhance opportunities for scientific research in undisturbed ecosystems."

Congress has laid out goals for the California desert parks as noble and clear as their dramatic arid landscapes.

The desert's yearly cactus bloom and spring wildflower show contrasts with its normal austerity.

TOP OF PAGE, FROM LEFT: desert mallow, helleborine orchid, sacred datura, desert tobacco, desert gold poppy with beaver-tail cactus bloom, "belly flowers" yel-low wooly daisy and monkeyflower.

BOTTOM OF PAGE, FROM LEFT: Mojave yucca with phacelia, golden fiddlenecks, chia, purplemat.

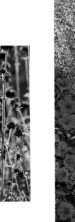

TOP OF PAGE, FROM LEFT: mesquite seed pods, bee on bladderpod, teddy-bear cholla with brandegea.

Waves of spring color dominate the landscape, signaling pollinators.

BOTTOM OF THE PAGE, FROM LEFT: dense brittlebush with barrel cactus and ocotillo in Cottonwood Canyon, pricklypear cactus, palo verde tree, beavertail cactus, hedgehog cactus.

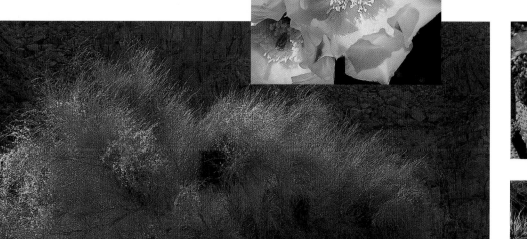

food-producing role of leaves, and mesquite, with roots that reach deep in the search for life-giving water. Elegant smoke trees line the drier washes; desert willows crowd watercourses with moister sand.

Out on the flats, creosote bushes keep their distance from one another. These fragrant plants ensure an adequate water supply by releasing secretions into the soil that kill seedlings competing for

Beavertail, barrel, old man, hedgehog, pancake, teddy bear. Their strange forms give them their names. Their flowers give them their spirit.

LIVING IN A LAND OF LITTLE RAIN Animals adapt to the rigid rules of the low desert as skillfully as plants. Preeminent among these desert dwellers are the hardy creatures that frequent the bone-dry creosote bush flats.

Life in the low desert must adapt to survive—each animal finds its niche. Desert blooms attract Anna's hummingbirds.

Desert iguanas, black-tail jackrabbits, and furry tarantula have specialized ways of dealing with the intense temperatures of the desert floor.

precious moisture. Creosote bushes retain their leaves through drought—slowly, but dependably, manufacturing their food under the driest conditions. In the worst droughts, the leaves, too, go; creosote bushes can live for at least two years without rain.

As a creosote bush expands its ring of stems over centuries, the inner clump dies, and the outer ring expands, breaking into separate plants. These cloned clusters of creosote—all genetically identical and descended from a single original seed—survive for many thousands of years. They are among the Earth's oldest living things.

Cacti rank as nearly everyone's favorite water miser. They have lost their leaves permanently, trading them for protective, shade-casting spines. Their succulent, green stems store water between rains, in pads and barrels and columns of ribbed tissue. They maintain one extravagance that gives away their close relationship to the rose family: fantastically showy blossoms that bejewel the desert in spring.

On the burning desert floor lives the desert iguana, which can stay active in extreme heat when other reptiles must seek cooling shade. The iguana tolerates such heat by withstanding body temperatures impossibly high for other lizards and soon fatal to human—up to 115 degrees Fahrenheit. From perches in the creosote bushes above, black-throated sparrows flute their clear song even at midday. These desert sparrows eat mostly dry seeds, and can get by with no water if they have green vegetation and a few insects to supplement their seed diet.

The sparrows' furry counterparts, kangaroo rats, have so mastered the desert challenge they need drink no water at all, though they eat dry seeds almost exclusively. Resting in cool, moist burrows by day, they emerge at night to bounce across the desert on powerful hind legs. These rodents live on water contained in the seeds they eat, and metabolic water formed as they digest the seeds. Their kidneys reabsorb moisture so efficiently that they lose little water through excretion: kangaroo rats almost urinate dust.

Some creatures have little need to evolve special adaptations to the desert, since they flourish here living much the same as they do away from the desert. The hard outer shell of ants and other small insects prevents water loss, while their shiny black color makes for quick warming on cool mornings. House finches and mourning doves avoid the

The efficient kidneys of the kangaroo rat allow it to reabsorb moisture while it keeps cool in its burrow during the heat of the day.

A myriad of reptiles populate the low desert. Shown here are a handsome desert spiny lizard and Mojave rattlesnake. Smaller lizards can be prey for roadrunners.

greatest difficulty of desert life: they live only where they can fly to water every day. Meat eaters like red-tailed hawks and coyotes obtain plenty of fluids from the flesh of their prey. Verdins and gnatcatchers, insect-eating birds living along tree-lined washes, accomplish the same thing. Of these four, only the coyote needs drinking water.

Snakes, lizards, and desert tortoises lose little water through their scaly skins, but their inability to cool themselves by sweating requires them to seek shade in severe heat. Birds, too, cannot sweat, and desert species like roadrunners and poor-wills (but not songbirds) cool themselves by rapidly fluttering air in their throats, an evaporative cooling method similar to panting.

Small dunes in the Pinto Basin form an open, undecorated stage for the drama of the lives of desert animals. Kangaroo rats patter over the sand by night, sensing buried seeds by smell. A tiny kit fox stalks them, huge ears and long legs all forming super heat radiators as well as

helping make the fox a fearsome predator. If the fox fails to capture a kangaroo rat, at dawn it may settle for a fringe-toed lizard—a reptile whose hind toes have a row of oversized scales that give extra traction in loose sand. Even if the fox bypasses it, the lizard may make a meal for a sidewinder.

We instantly recognize our first roadrunner, find our first tarantula irresistibly fascinating. Perhaps our celebration of desert animals rests on their success in living where humans find the land so demanding. Here life dwells with flair, with tenacity and character, in a world of harsh sun and austere rock.

BASIN AND BAJADA Flash flood!

Stand in the Pinto Basin, on dry and sunny ground above an arroyo, and wait. Here on the banks of Porcupine or Smoke Tree or Pinto Wash, the dry channel lies silent, the sand crisscrossed by tracks of western whiptail lizards. But up over the Eagle and Hexie Mountains, thunderheads tumble across a sky full

On a peaceful stroll up the chuparosa-lined wash in Cottonwood Canyon, it is hard to imagine the force of rushing water and debris that created this landscape.

of glittering lightning and dark rain. The storm clouds may disappear before canyons finally funnel floodwaters down to this basin.

Then it comes, a tremor preceding it around a bend: a trickle of muddy water that builds to a roaring, heaving mass of gravel and debris, filling the wash from bank to bank.

As the torrent fans out into the basin where it exits from the mountains, it spreads its power to many small, branching channels. No longer moving fast enough to carry the heaviest rocks in its load, the flood drops boulders and gravel near the mountains, the heaviest stones farthest uphill. Muddy water flows on, depositing sand, and finally silt, farther out in the basin.

After heavy rains, water slowed to a near standstill may reach the center of the basin without evaporating, and a shallow, temporary lake may develop. This lakebed, usually dry, is called a playa. Pleasant Valley contains the most conspicuous playa in Joshua Tree.

Each time a flood rushes down from the mountains, a new load of sediment drops in the basin. In wetter places than this desert, flood debris eventually washes downriver, ultimately arriving at the sea. Here, where streams rarely trickle out of closed basins, the eroded material stays put. Where canyons open onto the basin, drainageways fan out, seeking new ways around old debris.

The water slows, drops its tons of alluvium and gravel, and evaporates. An

tale of the tortoise

Desert tortoises *(Gopherus agassizii)* occur across the Mojave and Sonoran Deserts on alluvial fans, in valleys, and in the foothills, wherever they can find adequate plant life and loose soil in which to burrow. These reptiles are partial to wildflowers, grasses, certain shrubs, and cacti. They cope with the desert's aridity and heat by storing water in their large bladders and spending much of their time underground. Tortoises don't reach maturity until they are fifteen to twenty years old and can live eighty to one hundred years. Females lay clutches of four to eight eggs and when they are in top condition can lay two or three clutches a year. Shells of the young do not fully harden until they are about five years old, which makes them easy targets for predacious ravens and coyotes.

alluvial fan is born.

Watch for these fans on the drive through the Pinto Basin. Each canyon opens on a slope of gravel, a skirt neatly fanned out from the mountains onto the flat basin floor. Where large fans from several canyons grow together, a bajada forms—a sloping shelf separating mountain and basin.

Between active arroyos on these fans and bajadas, ridges of gravel remain free from constant scouring by floods. Here, winds blow away dust and fine-grained sand and jostle pebbles together until they fit into a near perfect mosaic. This flat surface, called desert pavement, forms an armor of stones, sometimes firmly cemented with mineral salts. Concentration of iron and manganese collect on these old, undisturbed pebbles, coating them with dark, glistening desert varnish.

As Joshua Tree's basins sink lower along faults, its mountains seem to grow ever higher. With each movement, each release of stress, basins continue their downward collapse; valleys like Pinto Basin and Pleasant Valley formed in this way.

Continued faulting forms deep valleys, the deepest (like the Salton Trough)

sinking below sea level. But as basins drop, floods continue to pour down debris from the mountains. Puny desert streams can't remove this sediment, so the basins fill.

Uplift can reverse this process, raising new mountains and rejuvenating aging landscapes. Meanwhile, each pause in mountain-building triggers a race: a very slow race between deepening and filling of each basin. Each flood erodes away another layer of mountainside. Each new load added to bajada and basin raises the fringing desert upward. Flood by flood, pebble by pebble, the mountains lose their rock to the desert below and gradually bury themselves in their own debris.

Flash floods can present real dangers to desert explorers.

Once numerous and widespread, populations of desert tortoises have declined dramatically since the 1980s, and they are now listed as threatened under the federal Endangered Species Act. Some areas have seen 80 to 90 percent declines in tortoise populations. The tortoise's plight is attributed to a number of factors, most of which can be linked to the effects on their habitat by the growth of the human population in the desert. Vehicles collide with tortoises along roadsides and crush them in their burrows. Feral dogs maim and kill adults. Tortoises that people take for pets pick up a variety of illnesses through human contact, frequently upper respiratory disease. Even if they survive, they may carry the disease when they are released back into the wild causing widespread deaths among tortoise populations.

In 2003, desert tortoise populations in Joshua Tree National Park seem to be in fairly good shape. Evidence of respiratory tract disease and other tortoise illnesses are still rare in the park, and population numbers appear healthy compared to many other desert regions. However, rapid urban growth surrounding Joshua Tree has many observers concerned for the long-term health of the park's tortoise populations.

The U.S. Fish and Wildlife Service's recovery plan for the desert tortoise aims to preserve the highest quality tortoise habitat possible, minimize encounters with humans, and slow the spread of disease. Like most endangered species, the fate of the tortoise is enmeshed in a complex web of factors that are often difficult to identify and even harder to change.

The desert tortoise may be a test to see if people can learn to live in the desert without displacing the very creatures that symbolize it.

Desert tortoises are partial to eating wildflowers, grasses, shrubs, and cacti. They do not reach maturity until they are 20 years old and can live 80 to 100 years.

of water & fire

Palm fronds rattle in a gust of warm breeze. A dense canopy of leaves shades a pool banked by orchids, horsetails, and delicate hanging gardens of maidenhair fern. A California tree frog slips into the water with a soft plop, and a moment later resumes its quacking call from the cool retreat of a crevice.

In a handful of places at Joshua Tree, stands of native California fan palms grow in stately elegance. These oases of water and greenery make wonderful havens for wildlife and people in the desert heat; they serve as landmarks in the natural and human history of Joshua Tree—as well as barometers of its future.

LOST PALMS Here at Joshua Tree, fan palms near their northernmost limit as native trees. Scientists believe that these desert palms are a recently evolved species moving north with the warm-

ing, changing climate of the past few thousand years. Still farther northward, beyond the Mojave Desert, killing frosts come too frequently for the tropical plants to survive.

Most natural fan palm groves lie to the south in the Colorado Desert, and the park's two largest stands likewise grow at its south boundary, in the desert canyons of the Eagle Mountains. Here in Lost Palms Canyon and Munsen Canyon, where water comes close to the surface, small groves dot canyon bottoms along several miles of rugged cliffs.

Cottonwood Spring, the fifth major park oasis, is an historic agricultural project from pioneer days. Miners or homesteaders planted its palms and namesake cottonwoods in the early 1900s at a natural spring, just as Indian bands before them sometimes planted palms at new springs. Palms at Cottonwood Spring today seem to be

In the desert of Joshua Tree National Park, oases provide havens of water and greenery.

LEFT: Native California fan palms can be seen at Fortynine Palms Oasis, and above at Cottonwood Springs.

The dramatic red-eyed phainopepla nests in oasis mesquite.

For centuries, humans have enjoyed the quiet comfort of oasis pools; however our very efforts to protect them now threaten the future of palm oases.

decreasing in number. Several trees have died of unknown causes, and the grove has produced few young trees to replace them.

At every oasis, a fault allows groundwater to bubble upward along cracks in bedrock. Only at Fortynine Palms do pools form at the surface, but we know the other oases have water a few feet down: palm trees can send roots no deeper than twenty feet and will die without permanent water.

Water determines the location of each oasis, but even at these springs water comes and goes as the continental plates of the Earth shift and shear. Cottonwood Spring poured out thousands of gallons per day in the early 1900s, but slowed to a trickle in recent years. Then the 1971 San Fernando earthquake boosted output to 30 gallons per hour—a reminder that faults determine where, and how much, groundwater can seep upward.

Desert Indians once burned oases periodically to increase openness of stands, to boost seed and fruit production, and to kill bugs ruining the fruit. Such management was natural: palms to the Desert Cahuilla people were like bison to the Lakota, providing fuel, food, fiber, and fronds for their homes.

Fortynine Palms has burned three times since the 1940s, and still-blackened trunks of trees there mark these events. Since palms grow only from a bud protected deep in the tip of the stem, moderately hot fires invigorate the stands, burning away dead leaves from the palms' lower trunks and clearing away choking shrubby undergrowth. With fire, few mesquite trees crowd against the stately oasis at Fortynine Palms. In the Lost Palms and Munsen canyon groves in the Eagle Mountains, floods sweep away shrub seedlings and dead palm fronds.

Water and fire give life to the oases; the post-war human development of the Mojave creates complex problems. Heavy pumping from wells, along with dry years since the 1950s and arroyos eroding deep into trenches, has lowered the park area's underground water level. Surface pools have disappeared from Lost Palms and Twentynine Palms. Protected from fire and flood by retaining walls and diversions, Twentynine Palms Oasis became so tangled with underbrush that now we must carefully manage mesquite growth. With too much shrubbery for fuel, a fire could burn hot enough to kill the toughest of fire-resistant palms.

Lost Palms Canyon seems a good name. Joshua Tree's oases once were difficult to reach, lost in the blank spots on maps. After American explorers found them, pioneers followed; we lost the indigenous management knowledge of centuries, a storehouse of detail about palm ecology built from the intertwining lives of palms and native peoples. Outside the park, developers have been drawn to the same oases that once drew Indian families, disrupting the fragile balance of the palms and their water supply. Exotic plant species invade natural plant communities in the park, changing the age-old fire regimes.

Rest in the shade of a palm grove; musing on the reflections in the pool may yield the intuitive flash providing the key to preserving the vitality of oases. Perhaps the brilliant orange-and-black hooded orioles nesting in a palm's crown know the recipe for oasis survival. Or maybe the trill from red-spotted toads in oasis mud carries the cryptic message.

If we listen closely enough to oasis creatures, if we observe carefully enough the life cycles of the groves, we can hope to avoid losing them again.

MESQUITE PODS AND SPIRIT STICKS

Joshua Tree's history contains few great events and great personalities, at least the sort memorialized in traditional history books and bronze monuments. Recent residents commemorate their presence here with little more than a cowboy dam, a few shovelfuls of rock piled next to an empty prospect hole. Indians who came before them lived lightly on this land, mostly coming to the park to hunt and gather food plants.

Only at the palm oases do we know of permanent camps used by native peoples. When newcomers first described Twentynine Palms Oasis in the mid-1800s, two Serrano Indian clans lived here. The Serrano were mountain people, their territory centered to the west in the San Bernardino Mountains. Twentynine Palms was their easternmost village.

The Serrano called the oasis Marrah: place of little springs and much grass. Water surely lured them to the spot centuries ago, and mild winters and shade in summer made the oasis livable year-round. Palms provided food (fruits, seeds, buds) and fibers to weave sandals, hats, baskets, and thatched houses. Mesquite and catclaw acacia pods made tasty flour. An occasional trip to Fortynine Palms rewarded the clans with cattail roots and shoots for food.

These people saw the desert as a good place to live, abundant with resources. Spring brought a rich harvest of bulbs and blossoms to gather for food, the sweet, tender blooms of Mojave yuccas perhaps the most prized. In early summer, gathering cactus and yucca fruits and the seeds from grasses and chia (a wild mint) kept the clans busy. As the mesquite harvest ended in fall, the piñon nut season began in the mountains, though the Serrano had to outwit squirrels and jays also desiring the nutritious nuts. Throughout the year, patient hunters stalked bighorn, deer, pronghorn, rabbits, rodents, and lizards to add to the cook pot.

Serrano people ranged from their oasis homes across the northwestern part of the park, but they yielded the southern slopes of the Little San Bernardinos to their allies, the Cahuilla. The Salton basin was home for the Cahuilla, a tribe of itinerant farmers and fishermen in the days when a lake filled the basin. About 500 years ago the lake dried up, leaving the basin dry until the Salton Sea formed when the Colorado River flooded in 1905. During these dry centuries, the

Minerva Hamilton Hoyt (1866–1945) organized several successful exhibitions of desert plant life in 1928, first in New York and then in Boston and Chelsea, England. She was founder, in 1930, and first president of the International Deserts Conservation League, whose goal was to establish parks that would preserve desert landscapes.

When this Mississippi southern belle married Dr. Sherman Hoyt she moved from her birthplace in the Deep South to California, where her passion for gardening introduced her to the native desert vegetation commonly used in southern California landscaping. Retreats to the desert gave her a strong

appreciation for the austere beauty and wonderful adaptability of plants that managed to thrive in the harsh climate. She also saw the widespread destruction caused by collectors who took specimens for their home gardens and vandals who burned and otherwise destroyed the cacti and Joshua trees she found beautiful.

After she was widowed in 1918 (her infant son had died in the early 1900s) she turned her energy to the protection of desert landscapes. In 1927, noted landscape architect Frederick Law Olmstead, Jr., recruited her to serve on a commission to recommend sites for new California state parks. The commission's report, with the desert section prepared by Mrs. Hoyt, proposed large desert parks at Death Valley, the Anza Borrego Desert,

and in the Joshua tree forests of the Little San Bernardino Mountains north of Palm Springs.

Minerva believed, however, that the best option for preservation of a large desert park was through the National Park Service and she began a carefully organized campaign. She hired well known biologists and desert ecologists to prepare reports on the virtues of the Joshua Tree region. She met President Franklin Roosevelt, whose New Deal administration became active in the establishment of national parks and monuments as an initiative to create jobs, and she soon developed an ally in Secretary of the Interior Harold Ickes. Minerva pressed for a park of more than a million acres stretching from the Salton Sea north to Twentynine Palms.

Finally, on August 10, 1936, after years of lobbying on Minerva's part, President Roosevelt signed a presidential proclamation establishing Joshua Tree National Monument.

Pictographs near Barker Dam as well as an olla and basket hidden beyond Lost Palms Oasis attest to the passing presence of early peoples.

desert people probably used the resources of the park more than they had when the lake dominated their lives. Today, the Cahuilla's Agua Caliente Reservation shares the same ground as the town of Palm Springs, an economic resource rare for Indian Country.

As the sere basins and lower ranges give way eastward to drier and drier country, survival called for a different life style. Without oases and dependable resources like mesquite and piñon, permanent villages like those of the Serrano and Cahuilla proved impossible. Here, a third tribe, the Chemehuevi, developed a highly independent culture tuned to the subtle nuances of the desert. Groups probably no larger than single families moved often, traveling alone from pothole to pothole, wild harvest to wild harvest, in seasonal cycles. Some of their rock art marked crucial trails and guided travelers to water.

Chemehuevi people were sometime allies, sometime enemies of the Mohave people along the Colorado River. Many of these desert people moved to the river, where they became farmers. After warring with the Mohave in the 1860s, some Chemehuevi took refuge among the Serrano living at Twentynine Palms. In the early twentieth century, most of the Twentynine Palms Serrano and Chemehuevi were moved to the Morongo Reservation in Banning, at San Gorgonio Pass.

In hidden rocky retreats, the people found alcoves to shelter graceful ollas, the pottery jugs they used to store their surplus. Spirit sticks, forked branches propped up at the cave entrances, protected the ollas.

Nearly all of the spirit sticks have fallen prey to the weekend explorers who overwhelm the California desert, finding their way to these caves and entering

them unawed by either the medicine of the wooden guardians or the laws protecting the park from plunder. Most of the ollas have bounced away in pickups, headed for the mantel of some misguided vandal. Today, within the park, only a few secrets still remain for discovery by archaeologists—along with more obvious mortars worn into bedrock on sunny ledges where women once ground mesquite pods and piñon nuts, with an eye out for their wandering children and the return of men from the hunt.

THE EYE OF THE DESERT In his classic book, *The Wonders of the Colorado Desert*, George Wharton James described a desert oasis as "the eye of the desert; its only means of seeing what it would look like if it were not a desert."

Oases have focused their desert eyes on a steady parade of human history. First written mention of the Joshua Tree area was an offhand comment about a group of "cabbage palmettos" (actually fan palms) spotted at then unnamed Twentynine Palms by surveyors in 1855. As miners trickled to the area, Twentynine Palms and Cottonwood Spring became critical water sources, serving as way stations for wagons freighting to and from the Dale district mines.

After World War I, veterans of wartime poison gas attacks suffering from respiratory ailments came to Twentynine Palms in numbers; physicians had pronounced this oasis the perfect climate for them. By 1930, the oasis where Serrano and Chemehuevi Indian people once welcomed a few adventurous miners had evolved into a real town. Homesteaders crowded out cattlemen. The eye of the desert saw a non-desert of swimming pools and real estate offices.

Mining picked up in the 1930s as the Depression forced people from the jobless cities. Many old claims saw renewed activity until World War II, when most mines closed for good, leaving close to 300 old mining sites within the park boundaries.

This Depression migration to the desert alarmed those worried about preserving it. A few people acted on their concerns. Elizabeth and William Campbell worked on salvaging Indian sites around Twentynine Palms. Minerva Hamilton Hoyt, wife of Los Angeles philanthropist Albert Sherman Hoyt, campaigned to save the desert flora. Largely through Mrs. Hoyt's efforts, Joshua Tree National Monument came into existence by proclamation of President Franklin Roosevelt in 1936. It became Joshua Tree National Park in 1994.

Today, the park is fast becoming an oasis of wilderness in a sea of civilization. Though the California deserts still resist colonization, one of the world's major cities presses right up to the desert boundaries. On the far side of San Gorgonio Pass live sixteen million people.

An oasis shows the desert as it would look were it not a desert. Wilderness can show people what they look like away from modern technology.

Joshua Tree National Park serves many purposes. It preserves a fragment of desert land intact, with its resident plants and animals. We owe it to our fellow creatures to save them such landscapes, where they can continue to live tuned to the rhythms of aridity.

We also owe future generations—and ourselves—such wildlands. Nearly three-quarters of the park has been declared wilderness by Congress—a legal designation that protects this land from all "improvements" and preserves a place where people come only as visitors. These visits remind us of who we are, and allow us to contrast our city lives to the freedom of the wilderness.

At Joshua Tree, we can look the desert in the eye. The surprises we see reflected here illuminate the heritage we share with the desert and its creatures: the passion of spring wildflowers, the patience of cactus and Joshua tree, the magnificently evolved bighorn and kangaroo rat. Subtleties and complexities, simplicity and detail. A billion years of time mirrored in rock, a thousand years twinkling in the glint of an arrowhead, a fleeting moment of color rippling an oasis pool.

These reflections glimmer with the spirit of the desert, shine with the restorative character of Joshua Tree. If we care for it with wisdom, this desert wilderness always will flourish, always will mirror in sharp, healthy detail our respect for this magical Earth.

Desert campers have evolved from a trickle of recreational visitors in the 20s and 30s to the steady stream of today's visitors who come to savor wildness and to briefly escape the pace of the city.

SUGGESTED READING

Arizona-Sonora Desert Museum. *A Natural History of the Sonoran Desert*. University of California Press, 2000.

Mary Austin. *The Land of Little Rain*. Penguin (1997 reprint of 1903 edition).

Lowell Bean and Katherine Saubel. *Temalpakh: Cahuilla Indian Knowledge and Usage of Plants*. Malki Museum Press, 1972.

David Darlington. *The Mojave: A Portrait of the Definitive American Desert*. Holt, 1997.

William deBuys and Joan Myers. *Salt Dreams: Land and Water in Low-Down California*. University of New Mexico Press, 2001.

Charles B. Hunt. *Natural Regions of the United States and Canada*. W.H. Freeman, 1974.

Edmund C. Jaeger. *The California Deserts*. Stanford University Press, 1965.

George Wharton James. *The Wonders of the Colorado Desert*. Little, Brown, 1907.

Art Kidwell. *Ambush: the Story of Bill Keys*. Desert Moon Press, 1979.

Ronald Dean Miller. *Mines of the High Desert*. La Siesta Press, 1965.

John C. Van Dyke. *The Desert*. Gibbs Smith Publishers (1991 reprint of 1901 edition).

Susan Zwinger. *Still Wild, Always Wild: A Journey into the Desert Wilderness of California*. Sierra Club Books, 1997.

THE AUTHOR

Stephen Trimble wrote the original edition of this booklet in 1979, near the beginning of his career. His eighteen award-winning books as writer and photographer illuminate the West as homeland, wildland, and Indian land, including: *The Sagebrush Ocean: A Natural History of the Great Basin*; *The People: Indians of the American Southwest*; and *The Geography of Childhood: Why Children Need Wild Places* (with Gary Nabhan). Trimble lives in Salt Lake City.

© 2003 Joshua Tree National Park Association

74485 National Park Drive

Twentynine Palms, California 92277

www.joshuatree.org

CREDITS

ISBN 0-9679756-2-X

Revised Edition

Design and Production by Christina Watkins & Amanda Summers

Essays edited by Sandra Scott

Illustrations by Susan Daigle-Leach

Printed in Hong Kong

Photography Credits: Gail Bandini—cover, page 12 (Barker Dam), 29 (prickly pear); Zandria Muench Beraldo—page 4-5; Paul & Joyce Berquist—page 5 (coyote), 7 (squirrel, owl); Carr Clifton—page 8 (yucca), 10; Jeff Gnass—cover inset (cactus), 28 (yucca), 29 (hedgehog); George H.H.Huey—page 7 (badger), 21 (mouse), 33 (tortoise); G.C. Kelley—page 36 (dragonfly); National Park Service—Cover inset (window), page 1, 2 (big-horn), 6 (oriole), 8 (moth), 13, 15 (tin, deed), 16, 17 (Keyes), 21 (fox), 28 (orchid, fiddlenecks), 30 (tarantula), 31 (rattlesnake, roadrunner), 33 (flood), 35 (phainapepla), 37, 38 (both), 39 (historic); David Muench—page 4, 19, 28 (belly flowers), 35 (oasis); Marc Muench—cover inset (tent), page 11 (climber in shadow), 14-15, Roy Murphy—page 6 (Joshua tree bloom), 29 (palo verde), 30 (hummingbird); Chuck Place—page 6 (lizard), 11 (climber, cactus); Galen Rowell/Mountain Light—cover inset (landscape), page 11 (lower left); Stephen Trimble—cover inset (palm), page 2 (desert, datura), 3 (both), 7 (shadow), 17 (five color), 20, 21 (nolina, chuckwalla), 23 (mountains), 25 (both), 28 (globe mallow, datura, chia), 29 (beans, bee, brittlebush), 30 (iguana, jack rabbit), 31 (lizard), 32 (tortoise), 35 (palm), 36 (pool); Twentynine Palms Historicd Society—12 (cowboys), 39 (tent); Larry Ulrich—page 9,11, (top and center right), 22, 28 (tobacco, poppy, purplemat), 29 (cholla, beavertail), 32 (wash), 34

The comet Hale-Bopp's closet approach to Earth is brilliantly visible in the clear night sky over Joshua Tree National Park.

Wally Pacholka/AstroPics.com

Joshua Tree National Park Association is a not-for-profit organization formed to assist with preservation, education, historical, and scientific programs for the benefit of Joshua Tree National Park and its visitors.